PEAR TRE[E]

Kalwinder S[]

A love letter of sorts a[nd ...]to the city of Derby and it's wonderful folk.

A second collection of poetry and prose, which follows the life of a Derby boy. Touching upon identity, community, culture and many other things that define and strengthen the man that he has become.

WARNING: May contain words that some people find offensive.

Cover design by Kalwinder Singh Dhindsa

Edited by Fine Point Editing

@FP_Editing
www.finepointediting

Copyright © 2019 by Kalwinder Singh Dhindsa

All rights reserved

The right of Kalwinder Singh Dhindsa to be identified as the author of this work has been
asserted by him in accordance with the Copyright, Designs and Patents Act, 1988.

This book or any portion thereof may not be reproduced or used in any manner whatsoever
without the express written permission of the publisher
except for the use of brief quotations in a book review.

ISBN: 9781794445864

@KhalSir
@PearTreeDerby
www.khalsir.com

"Remain firm in your convictions, but uncertain in knowing that one day they may change"

Kalwinder Singh Dhindsa

CONTENTS

01. D.C.'s Marvellous Jack Kirby.
02. Teachers.
03. 1874.
04. Duck: The Nazis.
05. Captain Slog.
06. Fanatic.
07. The Mask.
08. Noise.
09. DeAD.
10. Punjabi Farmer.
11. Represent.
12. Death of a Whovian.
13. Look A Singh!
14. Whataboutery.
15. Peace Enlightenment.
16. As If.
17. The Rock.
18. The Miracle of Cardiff.
19. Sweet F.A.
20. Chardhi Kala.
21. Tyson's Fury.
22. X-Hibition.
23. Scum F.C.
24. TownsEnd.
25. Derbyshire Way.

ABOUT THE AUTHOR
ACKNOWLEDGEMENTS
BOOKS

01. D.C.'s Marvellous Jack Kirby.

Nazi dignitary arise.
Crestfallen faces. A drop of the eyes.

Salute mein Führer and all things Nazi.
Derby County of England on tour. Germany.

Reluctant raised hands. A compromise.
Just following orders. Do not criticise.

The last line of defence, fist clenched by his side.
A goalkeeper back turned. Sieg Heil denied.

The Nazis they smirk until they catch sight of the one.
A head held high. A courageous shun.

The Ram that defied Hitler, an Overseal man.
John 'Jack' Kirby did not give a damn.

02. Teachers.

Superheroes disguised unveiled in hindsight.

Superpowers bequeathed through the moonlight.

Remember those dreams that left you spellbound.

Life's greatest heroes prowl the school playground.

03. 1874.

Eighteen-hundred-and-seventy-four.
Year of birth. A fabulous four.

Bloomer, Shackleton, Frost and Churchill.
Men on a mission with cast iron-will.

The destroying angel born in Cradley.
Ruhleben interned. Yearning for Pear Tree.

The Kilkea explorer from County Kildare.
By endurance we conquer. 'Every man lives', I swear.

The poet who scribed fire and ice.
The road not taken, his gift to life.

The war time leader, black dog – alcohol.
Pushed back against the Nazi wall.

He did not appease. Nor surrender.
Smashed Nazis and Fascists in Blenheim splendor.

Never Give In. Never Give Up.
When times get tough and spirits run low.

Remember the old boys.
KBO.

04. Duck: The Nazis.

Feeding his mallards at Salisbury Hall.
Sir Nigel reflects, ponders the call.

Nazi juggernaut. Golden eagle – swastika adorned.
Bauart Leipzig has smashed the world speed record.

Overjoyed Nazis have crossed the line.
The Flying Scotsman beaten. Malign.

Gresley's steam train takes on the mein Führer.
The Mallard the duck. That defeated Herr Hitler.

05. Captain Slog.

England vs Australia. 1981.
51st Ashes series. Captain Botham undone.

A loss in the first test. A draw in the second.
A Lord's pair for the Captain and Brearley is beckoned.

"I'll show you, you ba*t***s", Botham livid. Shackle free.
Brearley now Captain. Third test, Headingley.

Six wickets for 95 and 50 batting.
A galvanised gorilla an improved first inning.

But the Aussies declare 401 for 9 clear.
Then bowl out England 227 runs in arrear.

The Aussies taste victory. 2-0 up in the series?
A forced follow-on. "We can do this," states Brearley.

First at bat Graham Gooch is lost for a duck.
500-1 England Win! Chance your luck?

Brearley, Gower, Gatting and Willey crash-dive.
Botham comes to the crease. England 105 for 5.

122 runs required to avoid an innings defeat.
A stubborn Boycott is finally beat.

Wicketkeeper Bob Taylor quickly follows Geoffrey.
So on comes a new batsman to partner Beefy.

Botham holds on, with nothing to lose.
The Blazers still watching. A point to prove.

"Come on, let's give it some humpty".
Botham remarks to a young Graham Dilley.

The tail wags ferocious as Botham ploughs relentless.
221 added. Dilley, Old and Bob Willis.

England all out and last man standing.
Headingley erupts. Botham's name, they rise, chanting.

149 Not Out. I.T. Botham take a bow.
An England great. A sacred cow.

Australia's target 130 is set.
Aussies still smiling. No worries. No sweat.

Australia run smoothly. Reach 56 for 1.
Poor Captain Brearley another undone?

One last mighty effort. A final great push.
The ball's tossed to Willis. Oh what a rush.

Another like Botham. A point to prove.
Almost dropped after Lord's and again, nothing to lose.

Willis charges down the slope from the Kirkstall Lane End.
Hypnotic expression. Demonic bowler – possessed.

R.G.D. Willis snatches victory from the jaws of defeat.
A devastating spell. Eight for 43. No retreat.

All out for 111. Australia dismissed.
The defiance of Botham. A captain's spirit.

06. Fanatic.

I can't stand obnoxious tribal fanatics.
In sport, religion or politics.

I have no desire to ridicule and hate.
Nor waste time on the things they conflate.

A Ram. A Sikh. No Affiliated Party.
I was born and raised in the City of Derby.

07. The Mask.

On the day of his **suicide**, my father seemed to be in a **better mood**.

I had instantly **sensed** something **different** about him, but I just couldn't quite put my finger on it.

Yet, I knew that some kind of **change** was **looming**.

It was this perceived **rejuvenated attitude** that was the **mask** behind which
he **concealed** his **plans** to **end** his **life**.

The change within him was the **relief** that he had finally **accepted** and **chosen** his only **way out**.

The next time I saw him, it was sadly too **late**.

If only I had **acted sooner** to **premeditate**.

Beware of the false dawn.

08. Noise.

Noise to me – unwanted sound.
Unpleasant and disruptive. Quiet or loud.

Vibrations that travel through medium.
Pierce the head and cranium.

A space invader. Out of control
Bypass the skin. Deep set in the soul.

Do not be distracted by high decibels.
Listening to bull**** also repels.

Unless that is you, take a stand.
Walk away. Your mind's command.

09. DeAD.

My Dad's not dead. He lives within me.

From the start. He was always with me.

Years pass by. He still stands by me.

Until my end. He will wait for me.

10. Punjabi Farmer.

Proud Jatt.
Concrete flat.

No field to plough. No grass to cut.
Dependent on drink. Stuck in a rut.

Do not paint yourself into a corner.
No means of escape or room to manoeuvre.

Remember your roots. Where it all began.
Think of your faith. Not your clan.

11. Represent.

Diversity casting. A box-ticking exercise.
A sprinkle of salt to add to your fries.

Tokenistic recruiting. A dash of colour.
A conceited attempt to depict multiculture.

Diversity's nothing without representation.
Not being valued only brings deflation.

I want to be seen, heard and represented.
Not a token save face. Heart discontented.

12. Death of a Whovian.

Your time is up you've reached the end.
Into the sky your soul transcend.

Follow the light. Go in through the gates.
A flashing blue box. An open door awaits.

A seat on the sofa. Remote in hand.
Switch on the TV. Well I'll be goddamned.

97 Episodes – deleted, thought lost.
Hartnell and Troughton. To heaven they've crossed.

13. Look A Singh!

A Singh! A Singh! Look on the TV!
Watching James Bond in Octopussy.

Kamal Khan's bodyguard and main henchman.
A tall very strong, ruthless Sikh man.

Gobinda's a Singh. He's one of us. We don't care.
A turban, dark beard and an intimidating glare.

"That's Kabir Bedi", my father reveals.

But wait there is something more amazing, his acting conceals.

Kabir is the son of Sister Palmo a.k.a Freda Bedi.
She was born and raised in the town of Derby.

14. Whataboutery.

Sit down you odious anti-semitic enabler.
Enough balderdash and piffle – you labeller.

A danger to Jews, whose views you abuse.
Common sense you accuse. Worried voices. Refuse.

A once stand-up constructive, working-class labourer.
Now just an odious anti-semitic enabler.

15. Peace Enlightenment.

Jasvinder Sanghera she broke the chain.
An end to forced marriage. A lifetime of pain.

A shame on the community! A social outcast?
Arranged marriage not forced. This evil can't last.

Supporting victims of forced marriage and honour-based abuse.
No more violence. This ends. Karma Nirvana let loose.

16. As If.

There's some nasty folk in life you'll meet.
Who come across all sugar and sweet.

They'll bring you down and sap your soul.
They like to think they're in control.

They'll eye you up and down on the spot.
Then judge you for the things you're not.

I am an author, a writer and poet.
Not a **** stain to glare at and then misinterpret.

Toxicants are the thieves of joy.
Carry on regardless. They shall not destroy.

17. The Rock.

From the Edinburgh pluton. Arise Dave Mackay.
In molten magma. Solidify.

A Jambo in his heart of Hearts.
To London, Spurs his love departs.

A Derby Ram. In statue. Recognised.
Edinburgh granite. Immortalised.

18. The Miracle of Cardiff.

England vs Australia. SWALEC Arena, Cardiff.
Captain Strauss and England on the edge of a cliff.

435 all out. England bat first.
Australia declare 674 for 6. Reversed.

The largest total against England since 1934.
The highest in Ashes history. Oh no! What a score.

239 behind. England dream. Headingley.
Then quickly lose Cook and Bopara before tea.

The rain lashes down. Ends play for the day.
Resuming on 20 for 2. Now 219 away.

Dire straits for England. What a terrible start. 5th day.
Another 3 wickets lost in the first 90 minutes of play.

Kevin Pietersen, Captain Strauss and then Matt Prior.
The Australian bowlers are rampant and on fire.

England reach lunch at 102 for 5.
Collingwood and Flintoff. Keep the dream alive.

Freddie Flintoff, Stuart Broad and Graham Swann.
Keep Collingwood company until they too are gone.

Brigadier Block continues to stand firm and strike back.
James Anderson, nightwatchman now joins the attack.

18 runs behind. 18 overs to bowl left.
Can England snatch an unlikely draw? Leave the Australians bereft?

England battle on hoping to bat out the final day.
Australia become fraught as time slips away.

For 7 more overs Collingwood scraps away calmly.
Until he slices a cover drive off Hauritz to Clarke at gully.

Disaster for England. Collingwood dismissed. 233 for 9.
A monumental brave innings just short of the line.

A six-hour vigil. 74 scored off 245 balls.
Collingwood is gone. Stumble he falls.

Distraught and deflated he walks off the field.
Convinced England's chance has gone with him. Aussie victory now sealed?

Surely the defiance is all but gone.
Collingwood's net pupil is next to come on.

England's worst batsman. The worst in Test cricket?
Australia are jubilant. One more easy wicket.

Good luck young Singh. Give it your best.
Monty dig deep, England expects.

You may falter and you may fall.
Go out fighting having given your all.

The 'Sikh of Tweak'. They all laugh. He'll not last one ball.
To man the defence with Jimmy. Backs against the wall.

6 runs still needed from Jimmy and Monty.
Play scheduled to end at 6:50.

Watch the clock? Or watch the overs?
Spectators who dare, watch through their fingers.

Incredibly Anderson and Panesar refuse to submit.
Blocking and whittling away the deficit.

Australia are rattled.
England they have battled.

The plucky last wicket pair somehow continue to survive.
Fist-pumping every successful negotiated ball. Keeping the dream alive.

England finally lead by 1 run. 240 for 9.
Another step closer to salvage a draw. Hold the line.

Disbelief brings levity to the pair and the crowd.
Anderson and Panesar soldier on. Unbowed.

At the end of Hauritz's 37th over. 6:41pm.
Australia are humbled. A draw to condemn.

Anderson and Panesar have kept Australia at bay for 40 minutes.
An unbroken partnership over 69 balls with no loss of wickets.

To rapturous cheers the defiant pair walk off the field.
Elate.
Having saved the match and claimed a victorious stalemate.

Collingwood looks on with a bashful smile.
His unwillingness to yield was entirely worthwhile.

For the Ashes to be reclaimed. To set England on track.
This Test was the draw that broke the Australian back.

19. Sweet F.A.

The F.A Blazers they call us both in.
Explain yourself. So I begin.

"Break their ***** legs" a voice ascends.
I'm not having that I must make amends.**

**"Hold your heads high my brave little boys"
Ignore the foul mouth and his incessant noise.**

**"There's no need for that", I approach with a grin.
"**** off you ****. I'll smash your face in".**

**What a big baby. What a sore loser.
My young boys just defeated a bruiser.**

The bruiser now puts on an innocent persona.
Butter wouldn't melt. Out goes the nasty big moaner.

The Blazers are taken in hook, line and sinker.
Then criticize me for causing the stinker.

Why did you confront him and then raise your hand?
I was trying to calm him and then offered my hand.

The Blazers call us both out for being aggressive.
Gut wrenched. I didn't expect them to be so dismissive.

A beautiful game corrupted by Bullies and Blazers.
I have no more time to give to these Sweet F.A. haters.

20. Chardhi Kala.

Chardhi Kala is the Punjabi term for aspiring to maintain a mental state of eternal optimism and joy, even during the times of great adversity.

As Sikhs we have had it ingrained into us from birth.

Chardhi Kala is effectively a positive mental attitude. An ascending energy; to be in high rising spirits.

Chardhi Kala is therefore a state of mind in which a person displays no negative emotions such as fear, jealousy or enmity. Instead the mind is filled with positive feelings including joy, satisfaction and self-dignity.

But what if I told you that Chardhi Kala was a load of nonsense?

How can a so-called Sikh not believe or even practice Chardhi Kala, you might also be thinking. This man is no Sikh? He doesn't even look like a Sikh.

Well I'll be honest with you. I do believe in Chardhi Kala. The only reason I said it was nonsense was because I wanted you to reflect on how we judge others.

You see, what if I was someone with a diagnosed mental condition that prevented me from practising Chardhi Kala as my mind was corrupted by mental illness. Would you still judge me the same? Might you even abandon me because I could not live according to the Khalsa spirit?

Sadly, I think there are too many in our community who readily reject those who cannot fully practice this aspect of living in Chardhi Kala. As a community we are seriously letting our people down. They deserve better from us. So much better.

We are Sikh first and foremost. It is the Sikh way to defend and protect those that are vulnerable or who have fallen on hard times. It is not the Sikh way to abandon them.

I released a story about the death of my father by suicide. It's called My Father & The Lost Legend of Pear Tree.

My story deals with the stigma of depression and suicide and how it continues to ruin lives. I wrote my books to not only share my father's story but also help others in our community who have also been bereaved in a similar manner. The thing about suicide is that it stops people talking. That was definitely the case with my father and for what seemed a long time after, it also became the case with me. But as time went on I realised that the longer I refused to speak about my father the greater the chance that he could be forgotten in time. That was not fair on him, nor all the other good people in this world who have also ended their lives by their own hands. I refused to be silenced by suicide. Their stories deserved to be told. They deserved to be remembered.

Twelve years ago when my father died by suicide I could never imagine that one day I would like talk so openly about my father's passing, but I am Sikh and that is exactly what all good Sikhs should do. To help others amongst us who have also been bereaved by suicide too. I have found that it is good to write and read about experiences of bereavement. It is good to talk. It is ok to talk.

As I now do this I no longer feel afraid. I no longer feel any embarrassment or shame. I feel alive with high rising spirits and overcome with a feeling of great happiness.

As us Sikhs would say, Chardhi Kala.

21. Tyson's Fury.

Bang. Rock bottom. Crash into the floor.
Lights out. Knocked flat. Hit the canvas.

1 - 2 - 3 - 4.

The Gypsy spirit awakens on the count of 5.
Eyes wide open. The phenom. Upright. Alive.

The deadman he fought to overcome mental illness.
Fury now stands. An ambassador against darkness.

Rising defiance. Win, lose or draw.
Tyson Fury, the Gypsy King. Lifted millions and more.

22. X-Hibition.

Wright, Townsend, Adnams, Knight, Keene and Gresley.
Artists from Derbyshire and Derby.

The best the town and city has ever produced.
Exceptional in their field. Fine art connoisseurs seduced.

Masters of landscape and portraiture.
Mistresses of surrealism and impressionist nature.

Candle-lit subjects. Contrasts. Light and dark.
Chiaroscuro effect. Wright put down his mark.

Another great artist to add to the list.
Liam Roger Sharp of Derby. Comic book specialist.

23. Scum F.C.

We all hate Forest! We all hate Derby!
Back and forth it goes. The ugly face. Football rivalry.

Abuse on the streets. Vitriol from the stands.
Toxic words spat out. Gesticulating hands.

Sheepshaggers, red dogs. You're all dirty scum!
Coins aimed at rival faces. Bleeding heads. Numb.

Hate breeds hate and from the terraces it begins.
Players targeted. Different colour of skins.

The beautiful game's dirty cancer.
Calm down mate! It's only banter.

24. TownsEnd.

Unfooled by Chamberlain's appeasement towards Hitler and Germany.
Ernest Townsend predicted that all out war was a certainty.

Commissioned by the Home Office to use his skills as an artist.
Camouflaging Rolls-Royce Merlin Engine factories the Nazis would target.

To make them appear to be no more than a village from the air.
Keeping thousands of Derby workers safe from Luftwaffe bomber raids and despair.

An extremely patriotic man, who significantly helped confound Nazi evil.
Townsend gave his life in the protection of his town and it's people.

25. Derbyshire Way.

An English musician with a love for acoustics.
A female composer of electronic music.

At the BBC Radiophonic Workshop on various machines.
She arranged the Doctor Who theme created and
produced entirely by electronic means.

A street, blue plaque and posthumous honorary
doctorate in her name.
An unsung heroine the City of Coventry acclaim.

A perfectionist pioneer who broke uncharted new ground.
Delia Ann Derbyshire the sculptress of sound.

ABOUT THE AUTHOR

Born in Derby in 1979,
Kalwinder Singh Dhindsa attended Village
Community School – a short walk from his childhood
home in Pear Tree. He then graduated from the University
of Leicester with an Honours Degree in Physics with
Astrophysics followed by a PGCE Secondary
Physics.
These days he
works as a science technician
at Littleover Community School.
Life-long member of the Derby Civic Society.

ACKNOWLEDGEMENTS

Thank You

♈

BOOKS

My Father & The Lost Legend of Pear Tree - Part One (2016)

Punjabi Alphabet Activity Book (2016)

Homelands Revisited (2017)

Punjabi Number Activity Book (2017)

Punjabi Exercise Book (2017)

Punjabi Activity Book (2017)

My Father & The Lost Legend of Pear Tree - Part Two (2018)

The Colour of Madness: Exploring BAME mental health in the UK (2018)

Pear Tree Rambler (2018)

Pear Tree Rampage (2019)

Printed in Poland
by Amazon Fulfillment
Poland Sp. z o.o., Wrocław